The Arc of God's Love
Inspirational Relationships Justice with Love

by
Heather Butcher

Published by New Generation Publishing in 2021

ISBN   978-1-80031-128-2

www.newgeneration-publishing.com

New Generation Publishing

Acknowledgment

Family and friends we have lost along the way. Still, we press on to share "the one love, let's get together and feel alright" according to Bob Marley.

This book has been dedicated to those lost in the covid pandemic. We also share in the fight for change against the unfortunate death of George Floyd in the USA as we push on for justice against systemic racism. Against all injustice. We take a stand not just to bow the knee. Black Lives Matter Reading Forbury Gardens Summer 2020.

Ezra 3.10-13 Rebuilding the Altar
Sermon on U Tube Traumas Triggers and Triamph by TD Jakes USA Minister

Written by
Mrs Heather Butcher with her husband Vernon Walter Ray Butcher Director of VBH Financial Services
True Inspirations your Sweet Lady Butcher

The New Dawn

January after celebrating Christmas and the reality of a new year has come home in my bed of love. Do I really have to make a difference by way of employment in a British country so tipped upside down by the affairs of Brexit? It's time I exit out and get into the work place and make a stand for me, my background, my country and make a life for us both. This year has been an amazing year, the rollercoaster of British Politics in our UK has shaped our minds, challenged us, rubbed us up the wrong way. Years of the past have been dug up by the notion of Brexit to turn our UK upside down. To land safely on the other side of a Brexit deal that Boris Johnson still thinks he can push through, the birth pains of Brexit are more painful to our British establishment than we realised.

We all have had a say, question is now what do we simply do. We need strong voices for Black British Politics irrespective of what party we vote for. Let's stop the blame culture and start to listen to each other, less we fall. A house divided cannot stand in unity. What is the direction for UK and what are we truly saying to our people? The fact of the matter is Britain is a white country and we are all craving the attention to be heard in a white man's established. The mindset is being influenced and empowered by slavery white middle class which aim to rule over the minority of a Black British, wanting to have our say in the "Juggle Forest of Britain". One thought they were so great. The generational cures that once seemed to yolk our Black British folk have been up against the laws and the social birth pains for a Black Britain. Trying to come through and make a stand in politics, social media, film, creative arts, education, financial and business, we move on upstream.

Even our private relationships have been struggling due to the integration of such black and white relationships, only to have the dilemma or the reality of having to cope with the racist attitudes and behaviour in the family. Spilling to a community not going in any particular direction other than up against the racist debates and arguments of who should go with who? Who should sleep with who? to bring shame on the faces of guilt of how others are treated in such relationships anyway, as if we care minding our own business. The number of managers who bully the staff to do what is needed, is an issue to anyone's welfare in employment. We need to be pushed to be better beneath the surface of our skin. Mr Bully is out the question with disrespect. Trump's in the play ground of politics... The experiences of working for a cleaning company, with a very aggressive work colleague has shaken me to the core in a residential home, the shame of trying to earn a British pound pence and shilling is simply more hassle than its truly worth.

The darkness of personalities will always come out in those that have leadership positions. Thinking they are in control Trumps up to Donald Trump his trumpets blowing over USA The May day cries of a lady laughed at in Parliament, and Boris Johnson, a good possible Prime Minister with Boris Johnson v Trump – the ball is out with LBW and the Constitution to Justice. The struggles of women in leadership, who face the mockery of men, dare you to take note as many of our sisters are just doing it for ourselves. To take up the mantle of leadership is dare in itself. Who is a true leader, women will lead, as a true men protect the leadership of a woman. A Queen only to fight for justice and freedom for her people in the land she is simply Royal and she is needed in his life if only to smile by his side. The question is who is influencing these leaders who has now become our leaders for us to follow. As great as they are, as good as they are quirks in all, we need to know that are leaders are not only trust worthy but worthy of being our leaders. As we put our votes to the test we trust them to lead. In the hour of need, irrespective to who they are and what the party of the political persuasion is based on, there is always one that will stand out in the crowd. A leader without the qualities of being a follower simply cannot lead. Who are they leading themselves?

New Dimension

The plight of injustices in our communities not just in Britain but any country who chooses not to listen to the voice of the people, is the voice of noise with no voice to be heard.   There is no leadership, only discrimination as to who they think they should listen to. A sad mindset breading into our communities of hatred rather than love and respect for all. Having journey so far in life especially to build and now to rebuild a country like Britain after the political affairs that has shaped the country for so many years, has now to be exposed and exploited by their own political house divided by itself. We are simply not being able to get our house in order, for order to go in with every retreat, we resign in the public faces of parliament, the whole British political and legal system has become a sham to the people.

The interesting quality that most of us have as Black Britain's in a white country, we are always up against or not encouraged to be a part of, or when we are, the challenges that we are faced with determines how strong we are as a group of people in the UK for reshaping the structure and social behaviour of our communities in Britain.   Diversed we are still we cannot handle the challenges of multicultre in a community to bring hope not to just one culture.

The ink is black, the page is white, together we learn to read and write a good teacher once taught me – slavery mentality of buying us in the way of the slave traders of old now means together we need to move on and forward to make UK work for us with diversity and justice to all of us with heads held high looking to the one who sent us here.

–The sun will shine after the rain has poured from the skies of the British heavens over our lands as we aim and choose to serve our communities, washing covid away out of racist hearts and minds, we as a diverse nation serve others back to healing and wellness. As we all soul search our lives during the storms of covid, with love and peace appreciating the differences, the strengths the concerns, the needs of every community group in our country, not just the few that make the decisions in our parliaments to the Royal Garden of UK land of her subjects obeying her rules.

It's not about Black or White Britain but respecting the voice of all in our parliamentary and communities. Royal Assent with diversity now fighting fit for the best in Royal circles keeps every toe at bay as one continues to fight the issues of the Monarchy of racism. New blood as Megan with black olived skin just too tan for the UK, keeping her mind in check to stay alive is her highest achievement. The colour of our hearts now speaks louder than the colour of our skin. Speak now or for ever hold your peace – the voice of sanity.

The Windrush years making a stand as we reflect over our Black History, knowing we have a future in the country that once held us in slavery chains over our feet and hands. I simply hear the chains breaking of hands and feet so lets go further. Let them break over our hearts and minds healing the pains and scars of our history to bring the freedom to our exit plan. Together we can reshape our countries. Not with a hand fist of dollars and a gun or back stabbed by knives. Reshaping our mindsets irrespective to who we are to be free to do, to develop our selves not being held back by mental slavery mindsets. No longer against each other especially in those that were never born from the mainland of Britain. The promises of British notes outweigh the promises of what can happen. Gods promises are far greater, He is the promise keeper to all, to all generations to all back grounds with love and peace and hope irrespective to the believer or the non-believer – God will be God regardless.

Born to Reign no matter where they find yourselves invest in the time to be a champion a winner a defender of what is yours.

New Horizon

Our Godly women need strength to run our race – our destiny, our visions are personal encouraging others to do the same. Yes, my winning renewed mind has caused me to face up to my demons, my ugliness, the ugliness of failure, the ugliness of not knowing how to be successful in God. The beauty of the success of knowing that God is the one who makes all things well. A supernatural mind set to change my negative broken and week mind. Becoming radicle in myself over what is possible to become successful in God's love is a choice the best choice a woman no longer feeble. A strong Black intelligent lady gifted with talents and gifts to share with others. Any back ground any person I am in love with change- we are all in need of inspirational change – the change that changes our minds to challenge ourselves to become better for ourselves, families, communities and our countries. Open eyes of knowing and seeing that vision is for you to bring it out of yourself for others to see.

WOMEN WHO STAND their lives are very challenging and can be very unfair. So much has gone wrong in UK frustrations has turned to the streets. LIFE is more than this. With Knife crime on the rise What is going on?

PARLIAMENT upside down over choice of words when so many are without good food and shelter homeless on the street some women abused by men. On the other hand, some men having a challenging time trying to be good men and good role models to their children. What is the cost?... Another life has lost at the expense of a poor community with poor leadership meeting the needs of our youngsters the niggers of yesterday sing chanting for freedom "don't call me nigger call me blessed".

New Beginning

The seas may be cold – but love is in the air peace and a real chance to change through a better changed mind set. Having overcome a mental breakdown myself and pyrosis episodes in my younger days, lived through to this stage in my life to see my daughter accomplished my dream of her university has been the inspiration for me to move on to do better for her to have what I did not have or could not afford. Now mamma is at university two heads better than one keeping my head screwed on for my hed to shine – the light has been switched on – the dark room has a light of hope to share. We share in the diversity of knowledge wisdom and understanding from many backgrounds and experience. What do we do is the question – it's time to give back to others that need to see the vision for change? The darkest of ignorance is now open to the light of knowledge and love with others.

As I reflect on the journey of my parents coming over from the Caribbean islands of Barbados like many others, Windrush is the thought of everyone minds in a White Middle Class UK still trying to come to terms with a multi-cultural diversity country no longer on white terms alone. With the mix up of mixed relationships how can we possibly be dealing with racism at the extent of such British pride with the blood of the white man still over us even after the freedom of slavery

Our successful women in business all over the UK has arisen to our full potential celebrating with flags of international beauty. The platforms has been set high for us to aspire
Generations later many of us still have the scars of

slavery not just in dealing mixed raced relationship after a bitter break up but the shedding of innocent blood in having to deal with the consequences of mixed raced children very much hatred and scared by such a marital or relationship break up. How unfair when God says to love our neighbours as our own, or enemies as ourselves, be our brothers' keepers, look out for each other in the bond servant of humanity one to another how can a human heart be so filled of hatred to each other. Looking closer to home to forgive others from the pains of bad relationships, abusive relationships failed relationships, broken relationship, relationships that need to improve but by the Grace of God go I. Like many of us we are never perfect but day by day our eyes are open to the light of our lord and saviour Jesus Christ.

Three weeks before my 50th birthday I recall talking to God about my future. Where do I go from here martially, as a writer and as a mum in supporting others not only in search of their gift with God for either writing singing or drama, but more the extending love to our communities that are fragmented because of human relationships that have gone wrong in one way or another.

I was prepared by a special group of people not too far away from my home in the town of Reading, sharing the inner beauty of a Muslim lady she touched and beautified my heart and my outlook. To see her taking the time out to make such a lady like myself in the handy work of adorning a lady of colour like myself, surely building relationships is worth doing with others different from our selves. Does colour or faith really matter – yes but only to those that it does. In reality we are all human sharing the love one to another extending the love of human nature and compassion to others. The hearts cry of our human hearts needs to extend to others not just in the countries that are less fortunate in supporting children in orphanages by a few dollar bills or British pounds, what about the geniuses of love holding and providing for others as God has blessed you to do so.

 The dramas of life insults, misfortunes, and corruption in our governments needs to be broken to share the common good of our love and peace extended to all irrespective to who we are. I saw the light out of darkness as my thoughts was reflected in my first book Darkness to Light True Inspiration the jubilee of this celebration on our wedding anniversary delighting not only us as a marital couple but the sheer joy of the family and friends and community in my home town of Reading… where was I going it's no longer what am I doing with my life swelling in the dark.

My head is up walking tall not only in my community but in countries where my first book has landed me success because of the light of Jesus shining not just out rough me but in me as I constantly turn to him for help guidance and more inspiration to keep going. To what extend are you prepared to share light on your path on your situation in your darkness hour your king Jesus will guide you out of the dark and brighten your path as he has with me.

Relationships are important to me and always will be, the very fact that I have reached this far is a miracle for me. I met my husband I have graduated my daughter, I have become the role model for many others to follow – Not only does God know me but I now have a deeper understanding of who God really is to me in my own private life. Sharing my life with a man who himself needed the love of a woman of God I had reached the maturity in God to share that love with him, looking for God to provide the right man for me, many began to pray that miracle into my life.

It was June 2017 we wed at the New Testament Church in Reading having met on a Christian network to which we are for ever grateful. It pays to wait on God you never know how he is going to surprise you and make your life shine through the light and love our saviour. With open arms and heart I took this man to God double checking everything with myself and God, he came in the right time just after I came back from Amsterdam in 2016 after a second trip, the first trip to Amsterdam I was so excited to see my family – my Dutch connections from South America linking up with Amsterdam and Rotterdam I was so grateful how God had formed our family, Variety is still the spice of life, even in our relationship we don't have time to be bored and idle in the grips of Satan, move on with God he will show you a better life a better path. My husband soon proved me he was the one for me, still in the UK while I was in Amsterdam.

I found love after many failed attempts for other potential men to be the one especially after a failed long-term relationship where friends and family had the expectation of marriage. It takes two to tango is a principle my dear mother always taught me in relationships whether it was friendship relationship marriage or an abusive relationship it always takes two. In love I was with this man having spent seven years alone lonely bored with life but moving closer to God for my every need including my life partner, my Destiny helpers were making sure that God was going to answer the prayers and the desires of my heart to be wed before I was 50. The bond of sisterhood in friendship and fellowship a sweet lady from Ghana was my closest friend. She cried bitter tears helping me to pick up the pieces and to remain strong in the hope that God was going to provide that special love of a man for me and that there was no question about it, even now I am still in amazed at the blessings of God the protection of God over my life during the single years of my life having to cope being a single parent. The darkest hours have been broken now.

The availability to God means that he is available to you for everything and anything one needs in your life…I saw the light even in relationships. How could my life be such a miracle after the pains of being alone to raise my daughter to such a success the struggle was now over. My best has now been blessed to the extent I have become a successful single parent and in Gods eyes he had it for me to be wed. The stigma of being a single parent and unmarried can be so damaging especially with those that are supposed to support you which can be family or your counterparts in your Christian fellowship until they know the real reason why you are single and choose to be single to raise the gem of your life – your children.

The heart of a man is so tender unlike the strong body of his exterior and his manhood to be either broken by a failed marriage with a cheating wife. Well it was not long after we met in the romance garden of Forbury Gardens that phone call from the Christian network soon became my reality when we met and we waved to each other to say yes we meet up straight after work. Was this real, was this a fake, or was this going to be another let down. My confidence in men was going they were either in it for a British passport my body or just to say they can destroy my destiny by keeping me on standby waiting around for another 18 years sorry guys not this time.

In no real hurry to give my heart away one will learn from the past especially in relationships, you name it I had been through it even if no one really knew what I had experiences in the vicious world for relationships and the baggage I was so tired of carrying that baggage I was given up Ghana held my hand not just from a historical background with the tribal background of African and Caribbean relationships, this lady from Ghana was a believer and she was sure that God had the man waiting for me. My heart simply belongs to God to share my life with a man.

Being on holiday after I met the man that I knew I loved it was still early days, as soon as I got into the taxi DJ Cars was in charge of the road and romance of love out of UK straight into Amsterdam… "Hi darling I am on my way to Amsterdam at the airport I will see you in three weeks." His voice broke. "Oh you sound happy" I simply said yes. I am happy and I will see you soon wait for me. We kept in touch by emails during my holiday up until my uncle a ladies' man a dancer a family a man a good man a father a husband now a man of God in prayers for me my wellbeing as a lady on my own getting on in life.

It was Bob's your uncle. Yet again God came through for me. I shared and open my heart of some of the concerns I had going for me. I and the rest our family since becoming a writer was celebrating this achievement the parties and churches of Amsterdam, Netherlands.

Dutch pot of Love

Landing at the airport I was so grateful for a safe landing. One never knows what can happen as we take our flights to the skies. I wanted to remain a part of the loving family. Even though a part of me was out public for others to read. Did I care about my book? I was there to market the work of my hands from God in the Christian fellowship of my uncle in Amsterdam. Yet again God was showing me the love in my heart for this man. At a wedding in my uncle's fellowship, all I kept thinking of was this man that I met in the known Forbury Gardens of Reading. We took it to God in prayer. Amsterdam love flying over the skies landing with love bright hope for the future. In the midst of the storm the calm surely around – a turblant cloud as the nine clouds of joy is preparing to land on the heart of a new beginning.

Could things get even better? the answer was yes. Having met some very interesting people in his Christian fellowship, I attended a radio interview in Amsterdam sharing my testimony with a Dutch translation interrupter to share to the nation of the Netherlands, another place of significant for me and my family. This interview shed so much light on my own life even after the book Darkness to Light had been written to share the realities of being in the dark world of influences of Satan's grip. Trying to break free in one way or another…sharing some of the fond memories of Amsterdam and declaring the gospel as well as my book was a real journey itself to see the smiles of uncle's face bringing delight to me.

God has a way of sorting our lives out, the darkest of hours or sinful practices God will wash away in his blood in exchange not for money but for a new life in him. Blessed from the crown of our heads to the tip of toes, dancing in Gods house wearing the clothes and the garments of praise. What do we need to be afraid of we live in time we worship God in spirit and truth the blessings come down and in God's timing all become clear, yes God does work in mysterious ways just that we never know until He makes it clear to us or to someone through the gift of prophetic ministering or deliverance.

The "Romance of Heaven", families of love coming together a broken heart to be mended, a lonely heart to be comforted – the recipe for love.

If I was sat next to God I would kiss his face, or wait! Did he just kissed mine through the love of a man soon to be mine – all mine. The man's heart that has been broken once to be healed by a loving God a woman's heart who faced disappointment and rejection and brokenness like many of us, God knew what he was doing in his healing touch of mending broken hearts, healing pains of heart ache with love and joy becoming each bundles of joy to each other. By God's grace and love its only Him that can do that in our hearts and minds. As we share with each other trusting God to heal our pains each day in a cruelsome world face with racism and rejection of or own. I also needed to be careful eyes wide open testing the love of this man. We both had been let down and caution without running away from love. I had never known what the love of a man felt like was he real was he an angel or what it a fragment of my imagination. I had to believe more than ever before that God was in control and doing this for me as I wanted and needed. I was not coping on my own as a woman often looking at my friends in happy relationships wanting that for myself. I soon knew that there was no need for jealousy just trust in God that I will be taken care of like the others in my friendship and fellowship groups.

Like Jesus, his own rejected, him spat upon slapped to hung on a cross with humiliation. May we start to appreciate how he felt through our relationships with others who love us as well as those who despise and rejected us – cold hearts that need to be touched with warmth of sunkissed love of God.

Jehovian Jari was real not just a heavenly father to me and my daughter. At the time of my single life struggling with all my friendships, family and even myself up until I made that full commitment to God. In spite of the mess I had made of my life God soon cleaned it up fixed it and put the pieces together again of my heart and mind motivating me to do better even after archiving my best accomplishment a writer. I did but only through God I had simply saw the light at the end of the darkest tunnel of depression and a life that was going nowhere unless the light of Jesus was shining in my direction for me to see the light to which then I responded to.

Another chapter of my life was about to be birthed, I had given birth to my marriage even before we wed in Amsterdam the pleasure of the company for friends and love ones were prepared once we attended our fellowships one our returned from the airport Heathrow London at 11.00pm landing from Amsterdam, the body guard was waiting for me the love of my life the husband was waiting for me at the airport – what must have been through in my absence after meeting that day in the garden space of my heart at Forbury Gardens in Reading. A place for lovers a place for romance the romance of Reading and Basingstoke the heart blending together with family life, betrayal mutilation, control failed relationships the darkest of pits of hell through relationships was about to end. The hell of occult and traps and snares and darken minds with no home no hope no love was about to end my prayers now answered on the prayer line to God.

One becomes Two

Like Adam and Eve the relationships of the past were driven out only to make a new life together in the commitment of marriage, working together in love and peace both of our communities. Not long until we made it clear to each other and to our families we were going to wed it was 9th June 2017 we took those vows before our God – the God of the past present and future saw it fit for us to be wed, walking down the aisle with my dad a girl I was bravely walking into the church with my head held high knowing that waiting and trusting in God was worth it for the second time around for me firstly married now to my husband after the second time or him after a failed marriage due to a cheating wife. Still one will never know the circumstances of relationships in its entirely we are never to judge but to trust God for every need.

Who does not appreciate cricket – Watching the highlights of cricket Butchers, my name soon became Sweet Lady Butcher in a loving relationship. Cricket lovely cricket, did I get the email address right. Yet another blessing the background to my husband has nothing but cricketers. I am so reminded of my dad with my husband as he watches the teams of Australia New Zealand Pakistan India Bangladesh and course England. What am I forgetting the pill last night no. I remembered the doctor saying to me you will not have no children as you are past your menopause age for your body to have children. Pakistan the blessed country rich in many ways now to put our Caribbean's to shame with the knowledge that they are the champions of cricket as war breaks out nothing will stop cricket is the stand we all take to all cricket lovers, it's as simple as ABC, as we travel training our youngsters to be better discipled to learn something like cricket – a well worth discipline for family life.

A cheating wife with a faithful heart of love to her children is born to be a mother to love and to protect her children. A cheating leader like Trump to cheat the public out of justice and political votes to bring is own to danger derserves the honesy of a country to be faithful to the honesty, intergerty of leadership for black and white communities justice in the face of cheating scams of leadership, relatnships and injustice to lead to crime each shot a life gone dishonering our governments.

A woman is to be cherished not to be beaten emotionally or in any kind of way by abuse, abandonment or neglect by anyone not just a man but life itself has a way of beaten on a lady with a tender heart. The issues of life are always in the heart of a woman to make the song of music sweet the ears who would listen, or close the doors of the chapter of such injustice in relationships until God sees fit to move you one to better with him. The most relationship in anyone's life is God, salvation the born-again exercise to relive your life with God and his way alone not reliving the past traumas of yesterday, now the old has become new and old things and relationships have become new only through the salvation of our lord Jesus. Women who support each other are strong – why tear the skirts and blouse of other women in female fights over jealous and envy, stripped naked for a man to clothe them with his love and tenderness.

Sharing the joys of singleness by the seas of the Caribbean islands was more than the delight of getting over the disappointment landing on my feet on my home land soon after a break up that I thought was going to leave me on my own. The healing hand of friendship dancing all night with friends and family on that Caribbean Queen eating soul food of the island with splash of mauby meant that I knew three was more to life than what I thought it was at the time. Healing and deliverance were mine though meeting friends and family a new least of life healing a new focus to share in writing and meeting those that could help rebuild my focus for myself in the right direction.

The rose of Sharon the romance of heaven, "like a rose crushed on the ground" Jesus has reopend my eyes to a new love – He is simply the lover of my soul. He thought of me above all.

New Gift of Hope

Discovering the ARC Magazine in Barbados was a springboard for a newness of my background from the Caribbean islands. The windward islands and the leeward islands. In good stead for exploring the beautiful gifts of expressing oneself in music, writing and sharing with others in the cultural way of love and community, straight home to the heart of love of our parents I appreciated the love of the Caribbean Islands on our honeymoon.

A step up the ladder with God knowing that after every dark cloud there is more than a silver lining the lining of love from God to heal and to make amends in any relationship …Could I love for the second time around with the man that I had met to be now my husband only time will tell as I trusted God and open my whole life to God first and not to a man. Prayer was the key to unlock the heavy burdens of love first I needed to love my self enough to what I knew I must do and that was to love forgive let my light shine share the love of God and let others see that God was real in every situation no one was perfect and never will be.

The game of love is not a game. The passions of love to allow a man to even kill a pregnant lady with his baby at the British bus stops of Croydon to make the newspapers was the ultimate of love turning to hate. That was not me but I needed to guard my heart from love, allow God to love me and to hold me not in the same way of a man. God is not like man – a man that would like or should I say a woman that would lie.

The love of a romance of being in love and not infatuated by love but your love protected by God knowing that he loves us first, once unlovable to our ourselves and to others he has loved us enough to love others as well as ourselves and yes I was involved emotionally with my husband even before I said I do at the altar, the feelings of love was mutual until we planned the day we will stand before our God to say yes to each other until this very day on the marriage bed totally undefiled for each other we were not going to turn our backs on God or each other but allow God to heal as we grow together, it's more than a sexual encounter with love and heart strings attached for misplaced loyalties in the romance of love. Love is loving God first even before yourself loving others before ourselves loving yourselves as one chooses to love someone that deserves your love as God will choose.

Well to be frank to we deserve someone to love us or to love me or to love you well God loves us this much to send others in our lives to love us unconditionally as God sets the boundaries in our relationships. That is the true mandate for love keeping our youth inline to grow healthy relationships for a better relationship with those in our families, communities friendships and ourselves and God of course the ultimate of love. Love is particle not just a heartfelt emotional particle to show the kindness of Gods attributes turning away from the hatred that once had our hearts of a love-hate relationship with our community or others to destroy the fabric of what God intended us to have in community of diversity loving others as ourselves as we help others in a very true and particular way safeguarding our love ones and ourselves.

New Inspiration with Fresh Anointing

Guarding our community without the fears of walking to danger of the knife crime that influences the youth of our future. Show them how to love by respecting ourselves and others. The mandate for our society the song and dance of our communities as we listen to the songs of old Israel sings from the heart the community love sharing hope to a broken heart bringing hope. Israel keep it real please this town hometown girl needs the love to share the song of love in the malls as we exchange the kindness of our community.

So what is the way forward then what is the score then who was and is the man of your match. Are you well matched for your romance as the song of love penetrates our hearts and not just the gentiles of our bodies? Sex is good real good more than a physical act between two lovers of husband and wife but the sexual union stays with you day and night as the energies are burst into new dimensions growing you in a healthy way of a godly romance between his romance of his lady and should be protected being his queen for life with no wondering as to how long it will last but straight back into eternity with the God that bought two people together in the first place to be worked on as individuals and as two people as one in marriage sharing together and with others what is needed to fulfil the real you ….we were not born yesterday. Exercise your experience is always the best teacher in the game of love and relationships not just in marriage but in any relationship. Two consenting adults as x-rated as you like in love cannot be compared of the violation of the advantage of women with men in the bedroom the kitchen the work place or even the church with no appreciation or respect to the weaker sex – Did I say weaker sex or do I mean the stronger sex is a woman who knows how to stand her ground in what is right fair and just to herself and others.

Counting your blessings to have others around you that truly love and care for you respecting what truly matters to you. Closing the doors on the past allowing new doors of opportunity of love wellbeing and outreaching to others in new ways that matters to others not just from ourselves. Give and Take the true love healing and match for romance blossoming into the love for long lasting romance with your Destiny life changing life partner to grow you and each other. The freedom of choice now to be shared as one unit. Learning from mistakes in past relationships good and bad living for today and hoping for a better tomorrow for our younger youth to followWe are annoted to love more breaking generational curses as we are transformed with generational blessings. Gods prescription – his heart of Love. Fresh annoitign has come my way it's a season of power and prosperity to share - Master Jesus the pillar of my life..

Dance the New Rhythm of Love

I had always said that if a man was to lay a hand on a woman without the caressing of love making choosing to beat up on her until she was black and blue, he simply was not worth the tears. Break a man to make a man whole again is to expose him to himself, understand his manhood is not worth having if he is going to use it against a woman in such a cruel and mutilative wicked way against the femininity of her love to her with the maturing of her arms around him.

A man does not need a woman to destroy him, his wicked evil heart is capable of doing that for himself, if that is what he chooses to be towards a woman, to cry wolf, to cry the crocodile tears of how in just woman are towards men will only tear his own heart down to nothing. How does he value the woman's love is it through the given and receiving of his manhood between the sheets, is it through the amount of money she can give him, or offer to him for a successful life with houses, cars, is it thought the sweet talk of charming his ears off only to hear her nagging voice like a tap, or is it through the soul food of fish and chips or to find his match the rice and peas of his mother's hands passed down to the wife or the girlfriend to keep his belly warm.

The precious union of a man and his wife to be cherished valued as one, the value of his love to his wife, his bride, his closet friend after the God that is being served. To find your purpose, our purpose is to serve your creator your maker as one God between two people when two becomes one in the marriage that God has intended for you both. Was I living a dream or what is this a reality or what or is this simply the blessing that God has for me in accordance to perfect plan and permissive will over my life, over your life, over the lives of many that find love and happiness the second time around, Gods love is so great bringing the forces of attraction, love romance, the food for thoughts of our minds as wholeness of mind in holiness towards God and each other in marriage. A sweet bed undefiled with the greatness of faith, love peace joy gentleness and such like.

The gift of the Holy Spirit to season and to sweeten the fruits of our lips for each other in the kissing of sweet honey each time the moon shines so bright every night not allowing the sun to go down on our relationships, or marriages our families. Sun kissed sunshine's rays over the honey suckle and roses in the gardens of our lives, building the tents of love for our home as we get our homes and houses in order for the king. Did I say King…was Charles going to be my guest of honour in the Sweet Butcher's Palace as sweet lady finds the taste of her décor for her home. A Queen deserves to have a safe place to rest her head on the king's chest. The king of the Old Testament was ordered only because the nation demanded a king. A well love Queen for our UK, we dry our tears of our past as we lay our Duke of Edinbourgh to rest. We celebrate the victioriees of world war 2 yet we are still challenged by the scars of wars in new era as we try to make changes to our society – our lives matter to change for the best

God our king   for the nation of Israel and other counries calling on his name who has the last say our God mighty in battle. Still the sweet voices are still echoing in our committees and communities in my home town of Reading comes alive in Nigeria bringing the African and Caribbean folk songs in one community spirit shared in a diversity town. Shake that butt naked around town lively up yourself and be no dread as Bob Marley will say. Keeping waiting for the next generation to arrive in our towns my heart's desire is to be that grandmother one day as life prepares. The realities of the cycle of life knocking on our doors.

Mathew Luke and John still visit today in the newness of life from Jamaica to St Lucia St Vincent all are welcomed by name or by character reflecting. Coming back running the race of a Christian ancestors through slavery dropping the mindset of slavery from our mental slavery mindsets embracing the freedom of love shared though song and dance shaking the cobwebs of the past bringing a whole new aspect to love. Our cultrure, backgrounds, society as we harp on with love as we celebrate how far we have come yet still far to go on our journies. A man must be respected like a king 50 reasons for my heart to sing the joy of the love is my strength. The strength to love a man as the drum roll beating my heart to the timing of God's love and music in praise and worship in full surrender for forgiveness embracing the future of a real love affair with me and God my husband and I the king and I and the holy spirt as one joining as one. Looking after no 1 the district circles of a love around the country of our great country UK now challenged by the affairs of Brexit and EU. The romance was simply not going to end just because of Brexit and EU not when my love for my family and the beginning of my romance and marriage in Amsterdam, the seed of life in a sexy raunchy town like Amsterdam with butts and legs wide open in exchange for a Euro well for me I was simply going to keep to my guns at night and sing the old song the old rugged cross and I will exchange it some sweet day for a crown we are his queens in his kingdom as the kings arise to rule sons and daughers becoming kindom builders of heaven princes and princess as we serve the king on his throne – his name is Jesus. shining on his earth

New Eyes

The crown that can only come from my rewarder, the God of my life blessing me in the city of London and blessing me also in the country towns of Reading the city lights burning so bright to help those youngsters that are in desperate need for direction and a sense of belonging in the work place of the work of my hands helping the youth to stay strong in a challenging society. Was it just because of Brexit and EU that the United Kingdom was under great challenges until Theresa May stop crying for her deal to be the only way out for the UK or what there another way that we could go to appreciate the back door of the UK knowing that God was also in control of the affairs of the European Counties. To quite honest with you the majority of the UK had already welcomed the feet that was guided here another Windrush from European countries to embrace the work force of the lazy and the cult of the stupid according to Donald Trump was the way forward for the UK until such time.

What time was that the time when UK was not as great as it was spending all the money and taxations on high bills on wars and more wars never a just war for a just God, upsetting the Arab countries only to spread the religious hatred in the UK for us to leave ourselves venerable at the expense of protocols destroying our countries. As one door opens another one is close who says we all needed to have the mindset of the west. Did you not learn the lessons from Father Abraham who had many sons in the old testament sharing the love of Leah and Rebeca, the sluttery of Rahab at night the challenges of love from Ruth, who can question the heart of a man or woman when love is involved.

How was the royal robes and duties of the Arab monarchy challenged with the innocence of love from a princess, a child hood princess who is threatened by the harsh love affair of the deeds of his unfaithful heart to a woman almost twice her age to reflect to the nation of a compassionate heart to love simply hearts with every tear felt our country knows the pain of love to real. The free world, the third world countries, all lands are simply represented in the vicious love affair of mankind. How selfish can we be until half the countries of the world simply don't have enough bread to eat. The bread of life is their portion for the daily bread to share the love of song and music with the African drums made from wicker and coconut skins – The lions still roars in the deepest jungle in the affairs of man heart. The Lion of Judha his fight the king of the jungle

New Heights

Who can simply question the love of God in the affairs of man? We are simply in bondage of chains or simply delivered into the freedom to share and to express our love in word dead and action to meet the cry of our social needs in love and peace and humanity to ourselves and to each other. Is love really a second handed emotion where men and woman simply take advantage of others closer to home in our families spilling out the communities in exchange for hatred violence and killings with the knife crime to prove how much I love you if no man can have you I will kill you. The cries of the heart as number 10 and 11 count up the cost the expensive price tag of the EU as our country is being restricted to move on to the higher dimensions with God as he will allow preparing his people to march on and out of trouble in his kingdom. Is it such a high price to put the food on the table that he has set before you in the presence of our envies at the risk of others having to go without.

The affairs of Amsterdam was simply not going to come between myself and my family in the UK and certainly it was the spring board for God to put in to his own people around the centre of the most life changing event in our lives in the UK tables turning around as God hand is outstretched in the community and society of our countries meeting others of interesting background as he holds the purse strings to our countries by faith not by fate or by wicket deeds but trusting in the God of our provider to provide not only for our mage but also for a family members. Alpha Beginning Creator was the beginning of ABC the travelling of the sound of special children. A special daughter will always be special to her dad with the needs taken care of with love no distance is too far near or far forgiving and longing to see the heart of a father again to be reunited by love and peace the love of music to the father's ears of attentive mind to the heart of a daughter's cry.

The turmoil of parliament of May Deal May Day was coming to an end as she bows her head in utter disappointment for the UK how best were we simply going to make ends meet now that she had not delivered in accordance to her my May Deal to which was the biggest drop time for UK politics. May Day is still cry for our UK. The rise of the social media lobbying and campaigning for our country and the needs for our country in relation to other countries was apparent, October could not come fast enough to share in the Black History of our past to declare stand strong the future of our black heritage in a white country still members of parliament are refusing to listen to the voices of David Lammy Dianne Abbot, strong voices of the Black voice of the UK with respect to the position their hold.

The strong voices of a blessed Asian community coming strong behind us with voices from the Muslim world equally arising and standing to their call for others to radicalize and to be heard was always our challenge in peace and love we stand in some basic principles of love peace and loving family life man and woman educating our children to the marriage bed in the oneness of marriage without the threat of being deceived by unwanted terrorism threats on our door step, had the British parliament and government underestimated as was mentioned in the bail out speech of Theresa May on resigning.

Bless those that despitefully use you as painful as it is letting go is the beginning of freedom as you bless those that hurt you intently or unitality a community raped by others to destroy the moral fibre of love and peace by exposing the vulnerable with snares of injustice to bastardise and segregated our communities to breaking hearts to be healed. The inner cities of pain and bitterness will arise to give birth to a new generation of love and peace as we walk together brining change not by magic wand. A focus mind a focus heart and a determination to make the changes from within first as we flow out to our communities with the voice of love and peace and respect for diversity is our way forward.

Life was a lot more than Brexit she needed time to think about what she was actually doing the country and to the European countries of our families and friends and business, Fear not she tried and she never gave up with the dead lock and dreaded dead line the future of our UK was simply at risk having to be forced to bail out in resignation. Time ticking pushed to the brink of resignation with her hair tearing gout and many competitors in support and against her and her party it was just time to get parliament in order. Believe in yourself learn from the mistakes of the past the relationships of others in your work place or sphere of influences have you also forgotten that you have a relationship with your love ones your family your husband and wife or is all at the expense of Brexit.

Love is not a game give and take give way to others on the roads of life the straight road or the broad road which ever give and take and learn from others. The moral to lean is to learn to love others as yourself even in leadership position of authority at home in the work place in the family or in our communities. The Art of love or the ARC of love displayed in a community magazine over the Caribbean islands soon shares how best to love our neighbours as ourselves irrespective aiming to meet the human needs of our society in a loving way felt from the heart of love and not by legalisation alone. Our news channels break the hearts of many of how injustice our society have become because of the lack of human love in our relationships let alone the respect that is due to others and of course the one who made us all – if you dare to believe tune in and listen to the voice of peace and love with the steal pans of cheer at every cricket score you are most welcome.

Kneeling at the cross by my bedside I lay everything every weight that will easily beset me in life with the area of relationships putting first my relationship with God. Where was God in my life now, questionable like the three Hebrew boys I question where is my God in my marriage, my work place and where is God in the UK or had we complexity turn our backs on God. A strong sense came to me that politics was my area to fight for my faith in God not necessary at no 10 but form the privacy of my home, my conversations with family and prayer petitions for my country that I grew up in. Influences yes from the white community in the country but never forgetting the background of my roots of Caribbean and Africa not just to celebrate at Windrush to make a mockery and song and dance pf something so significant as our parents coming over.

June 2017 was that special and significant month. Not only when we wedded as one in holy marriage but the rise of sheer interest of immigration issues. Due to the failings of the Windrush generation, we were treated so badly almost a slap in the face by parliament in seeing to those that helped build the country. In the days of old only to change the conversation from Brexit to Windrush and how the shakeup of the home office needed to be taken care of.

New Blood

Hurting people from the Caribbean community having to leave their place of life and family only to go home to an island they once left behind headed by the queen the commonwealth to find the let down and the betrayal of they have been treated even now years later after slavery, the positions of the commonwealth being taken care of the invite to the country in the Windrush years only to be let down again, When was we going to learn not to trust the establishment to look after us after all this is the UK and we are always going to visitors making a home our bed we made our bed we lie in it in the UK until like the man in the New Testament we simply took up our beds and our backsides and walk with our heads held high like queens and kings of the ancient African nations – the history that has still yet to be revealed in our education system for our youth to know about in our schools. Or are we too busy teaching them about who to have in their personal relationships as their life partners as some raciest will say we are all the same – it a lie.

The truth is we are not all the same no two people are no two blacks or whites are the same. I soon learned in life that after I became a born-again Christian it was also for me where my strengths my weakness and my gifts sets lie with in me from the one that made me in the first place to help myself my marriage my family and the community of believers and the wider community in my home town and beyond.

Education, with understanding is for all of us to gain learning form others that are differed as we respect those that choose to live different lives form us. Is it an excuse not to love them in my view? No I will love them all the more embracing the defences of diversity to reach out to my community, kicking and allowing the doors to be open by God. The door of our hearts and minds to bring about a change for our own lives and relationships with others.

That is inspirational relationships for me starting closer to home me and the man I have joined with in marriage, humbling and bowing to God for him to take care of us and our needs in the county with all who shared in the boat of life in the UK, no longer coming in the 1960's but now almost at the of 2019 in transition to a new social dilemma in the diversity mixed of the UK.

The New Voice that Matters

Can and have we learned from the historical of our lives and countries or are we sailing the wild seas out of control for humanity, not even sharing the value of our lives with meaningful people to enhance our lives over a cup of tea. The pennies of the British Starbucks and the sales from Primark helping to help those less fortunate the light has now come help others as your selves the charity love of support and solidarity is the fundamental reality of sharing the love of a true heart to one self and to others be true to yourselves share love, and share your love with the one you want to be with don't live the lie to be deceived by others rocking the boat of your sanity.

Love and more love share peace that is the pride of love to respect others where ever we at, lives matter, Black lives and white lives. We all need love how you value your love is simply down to you, it's always a mixed bag in modern society with rights and legislations we all share in that humble pie of equal rights and diversity, money is not all I am always happy to move on to better and greater challenges that come my way as I prayer continuously for my friends, family, work colleagues, sharing God in many ways. Kiss and make up the real make over our hearts not worn by Loreal make up on the lips, however the kiss of life given someone hope and bright hope for tomorrow should they life to see another day. God reigns on the just and the unjust so who am I to judge but by the Grace of God go I.

A heart filled of love for others a heart filled of prayer for others, is the true heart that God loves as he does the work in the affairs of man's heart, woman's heart in his own time – its Gods time not ours we are only loaned the time of day to help and to bridge a gap and to be supportive as and when, where we can with the love of God in our hearts, forgiving others, loving others and holding the hands of others. Ss we represent Gods hands and feet to bring hope and light in a salty tasty way that brings glory and honour to a glorious God who has the last say. The silence is loud, deafening to the ears that are not opened to the wisdom of the voices of men and women in a society can drown out the voice of Wisdom and direction to our own induvial lives, we are remind that God is always in control even when we are not or don't know what to do or where to turn to in our relationships with others around us.

A passionate man is a man of wanting to change things, fix it as one would say knowing that God was watching us all.

The divorce bill is a very high bill not just for Brexit, how about looking close to home when relationships fall apart as a result of not investing in good relationships or at least building on the ones you have or around you to bring healing and wholeness of despite of the relationship you may be experiencing now. Life is perfect with God but with God all things are possible even when we are not perfect ourselves with a heart of God and praise to Him for all his goodness and kindness and love in our hearts we can extend that out to others in the best way and light.

The New Focus

The light of Jesus as shared in Darkness to Light book one, also improves our relationships with others around us, irrespective as to who they are or what they have done. Relationships best starting place is with us first, start with me. Start the work in me first understanding myself in order for others to understand me.

Our lives here in the UK must surely account for something, the journey forward on the seas of lived Black Lives Matter to make a difference to some one to bring hope. The year George Floyd died in the injustice of the hands of a policeman – the year that covid taught us how to love more and better. Surely the fight and voice of justice must stand against all other voices of injustices in the UK. If we can make Great Britain as Great as ever pulling the old structural and systems of racism, we can dream for a new UK with love and respect to all who sail in her. The journey of life is past meeting, the future by starting with the present – when all things can become new. Old things has passed away and all things now become new according to scripture verse

The past is no longer an excuse not to share and live a better life of hope and peace, love and helping others in our communities through the help our God. The slavery of yesterday in African or Caribbean form in Jewish or Asian of their survival in this day and age is no excuse for us to turn our backs on humanity. Is our status that much or are we using our status of life and the platforms we have been given to help to make others a place of reflection to also improve their own lives.

The heartbeat of love still is real in doing the right thing by ourselves and in our communities for others given no excuse for the evil one to penetrate our hearts with bitterness and hatred for others that are different or not able to help themselves because of life's issues. Darkness pit is to know that you are not help yourselves with others the light is to know that you are not alone in your frame of reference of your life. There is also someone bigger than your relationship or the issues in your relationship if you search you will find the outcome is better than you even think or imagine.

The New Mile Stone

My 50th year has been more than a delight for me to understand the maturity of relationships of all. It was an honour to have my friends and family at my official signing of my book Darkness to Light at the New Testament Church. Where I married Vernon Walter Ray Butcher a man of honour deep wisdom, a voice for the community as well as for his family and friends in the Christian family.

Understanding the story of my husband I appreciated the man for what he had experienced. The common ground was there to rebuild our lives together in marriage with the help of our God who brought us together. Amsterdam, Reading and Basingstoke our home towns meaning so much to me sharing life and experiences to many one would have been aware of now in holy marriage together sharing – God is the God of second chances in happiness and holistic holy relationship that are of God only if we follow his principles - the testimony's and the miniseries of our God over our lives moving us forward to better learning from the past leaving it all in God's hands to take care of in wisdom and love.

Loving my husband or my husband loving me does not take away our own individual need to be loved by God and to follow God for our own salvation, our salvation is very much a part of the bigger plan and purpose in accordance to Gods divine plan from before we were formed in our mother's womb, according to Jeremiah – Just we don't often know that at the time unless we are shown or a revelation has happened by God to reflect that is the case.

Money don't grow on trees as the saying goes, Well I knew

a God that made the trees and would also bless us elderly with the finances that we either needed to have for that time, or to give to help support the needs of a charity to which my first book Darkness to Light has supported the needs of orphans with the fellowship - The African Christian Fellowship Reading.

A New Vision

This vision in given to the needy and less fortunate became my reality once I started to worship and fellowship with my African brothers and sisters. Listening to the cries of the heart from the suffering as a result of the social climate and political climate, affecting the basic needs of humanity. No room for complacency, a real celebration of 50 years of African Christian Fellowship in Reading, the existence of this small but effective charity organisation extending the help to others in this way.

Being able to help has being a real privilege despite of our own challenges in the UK from a Caribbean background, we are still fortunate enough to be grateful and humble by the blessings of God, to help others in this way not just financially but also by way of services, friendships, ministry. Helping where we can morally to better the land of Africa as God is healing Africa a song we often sing on Africa day and national conferences in the United Kingdom – Healing is real in a practical way for our communities and societies no matter the country historical or political background God in his business of restoration to freedom, no matter what we see with our natural eyes. The hearts of the people will and is being healed by love, knowing that someone loves them until the day they die is healing enough.

Sacrifice giving sacrifice workshop and praise as well as a lifestyle of prayer made our faith a reality and not just from the King James version bible as we know with modified versions, today is still the bestselling book. Despite of the challenges it brings in our societies to which others say the bible is contradiction, like many others, to listen is the power behind to speech or to talk openly and to communicate with others in relationship marriage or in society we are always challenged.

I believe that though growing in relationship with others and with God, we can also reach our full potential to do better to make a change. We are winners and not losers, dreamers and not destroyers, we are people of destiny and changes, for the best and not destructive.

Being married showed me that not only was I able and capable of love and receiving love and the affairs of day-to-day life, in context to our marriage and family life, prioritising what God wanting to do for us, though us and for others was also vital. We could no longer afford to be running from fellowship to fellowship in hope of finding the one place to grow. The medicines of our souls needed to be healed I inn marriage in ministry in the challenges of our communities and social needs. The time out was needed for us to access where do we go from here in our journey with God and our marriage in relation to outreach ministry and missions

Justice the reality of Love

The Secret Barrister reflection on the process of the criminal justice with the rights to criminal justices states that the criminal courts are not, for example about catharsis, or giving the victim their day in court, or providing closure' (cited in Mehigan, 2019, p. 54). The process of any criminal justices in contrast to the rights of the criminal is also on the scales of justices.

In the scales of justices in weighing up the criminal justice system As Downs (2019) discusses, restorative justice involves facilitated communication between the victim, offender and the community and is one alternative means of justice available to victims., Criminal justices Focuses on the prosecution and accountability of offenders to which the criminal justice has a right to try the case once it has been agreed to do so by the system. Criminal justice and the process of such will not only try the case legally in any given court, however the case may be used as a way of example to others in the system for either educating or up dating in either high profile cases or exceptional circumstances notably the cases in this compare and contrast essay that I will be sharing on.

Packer (1968) describes the due process model as having less faith in the criminal agencies, such as the police, and believes that among few criminal cases mistakes can happen and additionally, there is a chance of agencies acting corruptly or dishonestly. For that reason, this is why Packer believes this model is useful as it limits the coercive powers of the criminal agencies and if there is an occurrence of any mistake or corruption, an individual has the right to defend them self. Therefore, the main aim of the due process model is to establish a system that an individual is innocent until proven guilty in court (Packer, 1968).

The due process model of the criminal justice in court cases especially in cases crime committed by under age youth - how should we sentence these crimes has been a thought provoking process for me on reflection. In these cases, children who commit crimes with a case on trial also needs to understand the legal system that their behaviour is un-acceptable. Cases such as the trial and sentencing of Thompson and Venables can be argued is it fair, did it result in justice? The trial can be considered as a model case for children who commit crime under the legal age of adult hood of 18 in most countries. However arguably the case may not have been a fair trial due to the fact that *the boys did not have a fair trial by using fair legal rules and procedures in a adult court.*

The UK has moved towards a more victim-centred approach to justice (Downes, 2019). How-ever, for many victims, CJS responses still feel limited. As Downes states: 'when the voices of victims are listened to, this "one-size-fits-all" solution of prison starts to seem very limited' (p. 226). **Therefore** Vitim's perspective as well as from a criminal perspective. Traumas may be apart of the victims suffering as a result mentally emotionally financially and often times families are broken or scared needing help and support. Victimology focuses on the Victim-centred approach that may allow for consideration. Being open and honest may be the victim's approach as to what happened as they make the case on the witness dock. With the support from the police, traumas units or victim's support units that are adequately trained up the psychological perspective of the victim preparing them for the trial is apart of the criminal justice for the victim. As Downes (2019) points out, term 'survivor' rather than 'victim'. The system also has the challenges to contend with to understand that members of our society BAME people, women, LGBTQ people or members of the working class – struggle to be seen as 'deserving' victims, often not given fair chances at the best outcomes

The system varies from country to country with the criminal justice being different and having many contrasts with the law by which each country governs and establishes their authority. In England and Wales, the criminal justice system is made up of several agencies including the police, prisons and probation services. These agencies are governed and funded by the government and have to keep to the rules and regulations which the government issues. Safeguard people within society and condemn and punishes those individuals who commit crimes is the main focus of the criminal justice system.

James Safechuck and Wade Robson are two men who came forward to accuse the pop-music icon Michael Jackson (1958–2009) of sexually abusing them when they were both children, the system has to protect the most vulnerable which also includes collective experiences of BAME communities according to Tombs (2019) to which procedure needs to be adhered to for a better justice in the criminal justice system with any hate crime.

Home Office: *Hate Crime, England and Wales, 2017/18 – Statistical Bulletin of hate crimes recorded by the police, October 2018 recorded Ministry of Justice (2016), cited in Scott (2018, p.153), (Home Office, 2018, p. 23)

Crime control model reporting crime believes that policing has a negative effect still shows in BAME groups with high rates of crime going through the system changing racism and corruption in the system – pressure groups Black Lives Matter more recently.

The Criminal Justice System also include Restorative justice. The victims of the crime may come face to face with mediation in a protected environment face-to-face meetings between all people involved, including the victim(s), offender(s). Therefore transformative justice which is also an approach and used by communities to unite to examine the root causes of violence and collectively work towards dismantling them. (Hudson, 1987), explains that we can start to re-imagine what victimhood entails perhaps empathise with the victim and how society can most effectively.

Packer (1968) and Michael King (1981), who have studied the criminal justice system and would argue that there were several more models which could make the criminal justice system effective. King (1981) has analysed the criminal system and has published a theory of six models which correspond to Packer's theory. King 1981 has suggest that Packer's theory still needs more improvements Packer (1968) and King (1981), agree with the idea that people should have their rights portrayed and given an equal chance to defend themselves through the courts and justice system with growing confidence. The 'National Criminal Justice Board' which shows that there has been a 2% increase from March 2008 to June 2009 in the level of confidence among people in England and Wales with regards to the criminal system with the rights available to criminals, my time at Oxford University during covid challenging our system against systemic injustice including racism.

New Generation

We are able best, helping the youth of tomorrow to stay away from knife crime, rape, murders, drugs, and gang culture. The evils that attract. There is hope for them, education programmes and more re-education programs to help keep our youth in line though sports. The passions form my husband in sharing his heart for the youth meant I was not going to get in the way or in his way. To allow God to help him shape him and mould him for the ministry of the young people not just in fellowships that we were a part of our Christian faith but also helping the community where needed, his love for cricket came to everyone's attention through the social media and local newspaper.

A spiritual son in the New Testament opened his heart I was mother to him in my heart never having the blessing of son I soon took a shine to him in this way and encouraged him to continue to do the drama classes in the fellowship in order to express his heart as well as this faith from a very real particle way.

Every family life is different all needs to be respected. After all a lot of our life experiences we have no control over and is put on us or we have gone though as a result of someone else. The healing process for a deeper relationship with yourselves and others starts with you and God for the desired relationship that God want you to have with him and with others -vertical and horizontal relationships. It's a surgery of the heart to know you have seen the light out of a dark place and still not able to rebuild or build relationships with others.

New Zone of Power

Many relationships are formed for many reasons, many friendships, many friends, few friends. The spirit of hatred, bitterness, as a result of the brokenness that many of feel or have experiences needs that special hands of love from God above in the form of healing and healthy relationships and friendships with Time as the healer to enjoy life to move on a step closer to your chosen or desired purpose from God. No relationship taken the place of God no goal in life taken the place where God should be in our hearts to help us to succeed.

The stepping stone of using others to build one's empire is soon to be smashed down, as we see too often in the political world of challenging relationships and mis trust in political circles to bread the corruption that many have in offices. In favour of a vote, for power at the expense of the people. We are not each other's success ladders, however the ladder of success up to heaven like Jacobs ladder the angles from above will defend you on our journey up to God for your success with him, for the purpose that he has for you. With God you are a winner no matter the journey of the challenges.

The egos of our lives are soon humbled by the realities of how much we need our God, male and female to refocus on the priories of our lives and what really matters. I examine my own heart and question what really makes a marriage work? Is it the prayers up to God? The sexual union with a marriage bed undefiled? Is it our worship to God? Is it the readiness and the preparations of our hearts body soul and mind? Is it the money, the material possessions that we have or don't have? Is it the status and the platforms we have? Can God be setting up our society whether we believe in

Him or not against humanity that is selfish building our own empires?

The humbles to our God breaking the egos and the pride of man and woman in marriage and relationship can only be done by God himself, God wants our hearts and nothing else only to position us with the right people for us to grow and to help others on their path of righteousness to a successful journey. For he knows the plans for you to give me a hope and a future and not to harm you no matter the challenge.

God is no respect of persons as we turn the other cheek in the face of adversity and challenges, we then and only then know how to love others as God has loved us and to show that by the way we demonstrate to others around us leaving a long-lasting legacy and blessings for the next generation to follow and to admire. Breaking the generational cures over our families by the way we treat others with love and respect as well as the hand of prayer to take us out of the pit of despair. The Joseph Story the coat of many colours a well family favourite is a lesson learned in all our families when sharing the vision of what God has for us or the testimony of what he has already done and the faith to keep going to move on with him all the way in his chosen unique assignment that he has for you.

Be it be politics in government, be it be business, be it finances, be it teaching and education be it society and community, God is very real and is seeing to your calling in however way he wants you to influence and change others around you and your community, not just of believers but those that are also non-believers, as they have chosen to rightly or wrongly.

We have choices to make. Been there, done that, worn the T shirt, I now have a new garment of praise to show for it all as I travel with God in a new deeper dimension in relationships including marriage and most of all my relationship with him. Private and confidential in his eyes of love for me and his loving kindliness to all of us as human beings in need of love from a God.

When the pride of a man or woman stands in the way of facing up to one's skeletons in the closet with God, allowing God to show you who really are before him its worth having a change of heart. It's a man's world but not without a woman for some.

The issues of the heart. Life one leads comes from the issues of the heart, life and death is always in the power of the tongue to correct, to heal, to pull down, to shatter the plans of a lying or deceitful tongue with quiet lips and tongues but a deceitful. One can never turn the clock back who would want to. In life when others take you for granted and misunderstand or mis represent you the mistrust and the gap just grow apart no longer in tune with each other's heart space of the romance and love.

A New Era

- The Fighters, The Freedom Fighter, The Warriors, The Kings and Queens of our Motherland Africa

George Floyd we relive our hearts to rebuild our communities as we face the irony of should this have happened. To stand attention to racism, not just to black folk but the Chinese population with Covid how cold hearts of the joker of Donald Trump trumping his horns. How did that make his voice known at a drop of a vote. Alabama Georgia and beyond cry the bitter tears of his failures only to the Freedom to Refocus our lives with bended knees to respect a race.

God who made those in parliament to make decisions. A new Era of breaking the chains of racial divided is passion of Gods heart, only to bow to a God who made black and white folk. Humble hearts for life as we surrender to say to our maker we need better. The enemies of those who seek war hate and destruction of communities with no love in their hearts must come to an end.

New Direction Forward

The food for thought in keeping the sanity of heart and mind clean for the service of God is not an excuse for the suffering of man or woman in any relationship for God.

The sacrifice of giving to women to men an men to women in days of old and offering sacrifice in the buildings of temples is now in exchange for the sacrifice of prayer and praise and worship from a true heart of worship knowing that we are not perfect human beings but in need of the help of Gods spirit to flow in our hearts and minds to make amends to marriages relationships and families that challenged us on a daily basis as well as the challenges from the world and Satan to put strain our lives.

We cast our burdens on Jesus the close friend stick closet than a brother husband sister mother or any other relationship. There is no escape but God is behind us before us over us and our high priest for our relationships knowing that God has all the affairs of mankind in his sight and vison. His mind is to reveal his mind to us through relationships and also through the work of our hands as well as through the characters of the bile.

New family of Love

The family unit is the bedrock for our society, our Christian society that is challenged by modern life and those that are not Christians for whatever the reasons are. Do we need to revisit our own roots of our own families not just from a historical and social view point, however we view our lives, marriages and families God is knocking on the doors of our hearts.

We may need to make amends and apologise, we may need to pick up the phone to say hello how are you, we may need to be fair and let go putting the past behind you, we may need to find out why and what has happened for the break down in our communication with each other not just a marital communication, we may need to simply ask ourselves where is God or more to the fact where am I with God in my relationships with others more importantly the relationship with God and me to even help me move on and grow in my purpose with God which of course is serve him in spirit and in truth in the service of family marriage friends and our social communities in the best way that is pleasing and right before a holy God that knows all things and all heart issues where the issues of life flows.

Don't allow the love you're your heart to be mis placed by ill feelings of unhealthy emotions to pull you down to the pits of despair or depression as to which was covered in my first book Darkness to Light. Having found a good relationship with God and he with me I am constantly growing in his love peace and joy breaking the heavy burdens of generational traditions from family members going around in cycles not achieving anything but heart ache fuss and pointless conversations that only adds more strain on one's life and the relationship of family marriages and friendships.

New Race to Run

The wealthiest of families including our Royal family has been challenged of now to see the blessing and the challenges of a royal queen. Mixed blessings or a mixed challenged marriage with the blessing and sentencing of love to be soon to be blooming in family life for others to be observing. r. Surely love is worth the standing for what is right what Is noble what is fair what is protective and honourable not just in marriage but also in our society learning form the past moving to the future of lives in a country so filled with diversity and respect for others irrespective to what we think is right or wrong…

The right thing is to simply love and more love in hearts in word and in dead and in our behaviour towards each other spilling into the streets of our communities without the culture of knives and gang cultures to destroy the heart of human love that they themselves also crave for. The ecstasy of love is never be compared from the ecstasy of a true love a true romance of oneself with you and God understanding what true love is really all about or is it just the second handed emotions that all take for garneted to end up dead by the bus stop from a university with parents having to live the pain in their hearts as with Steven Lawrence and many others that has become victims of the injustice and hatred in our society due the knives and the culture of gangs, How many are we going to lose in our youth because of the lack of love being shared not only in their own hearts but also for them.

New Dreams for Bright Hopes

The battles of being a single parent an absent father, a mother unable to cope, the stigma of receiving government money or in the employment that you rather do without, the trauma of carrying a rape child or having an abortion or falling victim of an abusive relationship or manager at work the survival for life the jungle of life -still the lion of the jungle the real lion of Juda will roar as loud more louder than Satan who is also roaring sound like a lion to devour your heart mind and soul and our relationships through the hatred and bitterness and the pressure of our society.

We need to take responsibility no loner to blame or society for the actions and the consequences but look inwards to find the love in our hearts that we all have to love our selves first to love others and our husbands and wives to rebuild the families the modern core to our sociality not leaving alone to the powers of parliament or any other government to take hold of our own responsibilities where we have failed ourselves for the buck to be passed to others to take care of and still complain.

We are treasure in earthen vessels all belonging to God the just and the unjust the Christians and the non-all responsible to share the love of human nature to others, if there is no love in your heart lean to love it's not always a passive and quite voice. Declare you're your love in action for others in social action and wellbeing for others as well as yourselves. Heal the pains of our broken hearts in our communities by sharing love the youth of today are desperate for that love adults and the elderly the labour of love is the love that God has for us as we show others how to love as we love we will be in return be loved as we leave our legacy behind for the next generation to follow or to take up from. A day of freedom a freedom dance celebrating the past hurts of relationships a gem of the ARC of love is to listen to the heart of the cry as we sail the seas in the love boat for marriages family communities and social concerns where ever we come from.

Renewed Faith

Keeping the faith, party faith in our communities, of dance worship to our God. A better today, brighter tomorrow, a better tomorrow is our hope. Creating a better future for all. Love is a not a game of love set and match on the centre court in space landing on Venus. Your love, my love for my marriage with a man sent to me and I to him sharing the views of a challenging and changing life in the UK. We of ourselves cannot change UK but we both know a God who looks after and watch over the affairs of our lives irrespective to where we live his love is real and we have chosen not to sail the wild seas no more without a compass or direction from the ones who made the seas. In view of Windrush cold, rainy, dull days of sunny UK, when compared to the blue shores of the love islands of sunshine missed so dearly.

We respect our generations past our future generations for a bright tomorrow to carry the mantel of love and not hate to others to bring true change to a challenging UK filled with the multi culture and diversity of life – it's always an interesting place to live and learn who knows our doors are always open for opportunity for others from other main lands or is Brexit closing the doors. Regardless to this where we travel where ever we come from we all in need in the search of love from God through others – it's worth sharing. Deuteronomy blessings instead of cures to follow.

The New Recipe For Love

Sunflower oil massage oil peppermint tea rosemary lamb succulent potatoes and stuffed peppers spiced and chillies hot chillies and peppers on a bed of rocket salad one red rose one plate not too much on the plate plenty of refreshing still water, a hot steamy bath one sauna a month breakfast of love throughout the day supper of chats a night of romance hot and steamy relations after the man of the match has scored your heart to catch you as you fall. Aiming high with potential as God is our focus hot saunas the sweat box of all impurities to modern life occasional visit back to your honey moon suit.... the Sunkist beaches of the islands to rock our boat in the ARC of love closing the business of life every day with a glass of white wine .... the inspirational recipe for love.

New Sailing on New Shores

Sailing in Bridgetown on our honey moon in Barbados the visitation of the Spanish on our honeymoon.

The Islands appreciate the arts and crafts of many talented and gifted people young and old. A culture of diversity and life in the sunshine tropics of our parents with honour and respects to our Windrush Generation 2019 as we celebrate our Black History Month every October we surely do have a future a true complement to ARC Magazine and CBC Radio Station celebrating Bajan life in Barbados Bridge town at the Harbour and Parliamentary offices of Bridgetown Barbados. Never forgetting our backgrounds in respect of Windrush and Black History Month 2019

The Deception of the Voodoo god -
the recipe from Witchcraft to Christ

1 black magic portion to taste

1 bottle of protection with the curses against the evil with a bewitching spells at the front door.

1 voodoo doll to spell the magic of love and desire of lust of evil eyes to prey good luck.

1 occultist wash with bewitching spells to forget your family issues – We sing. "Who has the final say" as we rebuild the altar according to Ezra stones of worship cry to God for the deliverance of evils.

New Sounds of Blackness

The octave of sound of music of our historical backgrounds shapes our communities for love. Love and hate crimes all round our social diversity mixed pot is brought to light by the sudden fights on the streets of London UK sharing the hatred of black-on-black crimes fuel by racists organisations, drug gangs and gun cultured influences from New York we cry the tears of Africa and weep the sorrows from the Caribbean islands each year the October missions is to save our people.

From Black History in October to the rise of Black Empowerment through our Pentecostal churches investing in ourselves in our communities stepping into a whole new dimension from the past history of pain to the bright future of knowing that we can do all things, as Christians through Jesus who is our strength. Yet still the shame of segregation from the old gospel negros of USA and Alabama only to listen from one generation to another the speeches of our hero Obama who has made it to the top of his successes to be the role model admirable to many who want to aspire to the top. Be it politics, education, legal affairs or preachers or simply keeping our communities in order we all aim together the X of Malcom is not a mistake, no X in past relationships no X for mistake for aiming to resolve the issues in our own community that tries to challenges us.

The mindset of or white counter parts main land Europe challenging the views of Brexit in UK our political climate has changed like the sunshine and the rains blowing from east to west. When will east meet west at all cost a jet ride away to make the deals of the golden handshakes so we can travel the skies from east to west only to go bust like the balloon. What is man black or white? A brain waiting to explode to the full potential the grey matter of our cells no longer sick in a cell with prison bars and slam door behind the walls of freedom to right the manuscripts of experiences from UK jail for drug crime.

The lessons learned after five years how wise has one become these days to only come out with the university degree from a prison cell at the expense of neglecting the child, the family your love ones your freedom at a drop of a hat to bury your true potential for others to unveil the truth behind the mysteries of your darkest hour to sing the souls of freedom to the alter of victory. The songs of beauty the Sista with soul her voice is beauty her love is pure she cries for the love of her heart who am I just where do I belong where is my true identify.

Courage to Move On

Going back to the Spanish shores and Latin roots of dance from Spanish Town to Latin America, Port of Spain to the Columbus islands we find our Black History Movement for Respiratory Justice celebrates our victories as a black community empowered to bring out the potentials in all of us both black and white, our Asian backgrounds all religions transcending that our human nature is all in need of love and peace without argument or question. How dare a home is used as a place of violence to disturb the peace of love to our lives. In darkness we once walked, the light now shone to bring about change to dark community.

The screaming voices of needing love in our communities is very real. The global movement at our Cafes need to share the love of music to awake your cities to life sharing the cross cultural and leaning from others as we move on and forward. Allowing our differences to shape what we have to bring communities together with understanding and wisdom. How can we best understand our differences, our cultural differences is it through relationships, families integrating or simply educating and applying the wisdom with forgiveness of heart to others or all of the above.

Politics and our social challenges are only the beginning to a spring board of the change that we all need starting with the UK of our Brexit challenged with the main land of our European colony from past slavery ownership to a brighter liberated mixed Afro Caribbean background Europe as the challenges of the Johnsons march forward to make the change stating with Boris Johnson. My historical name of Johnson from my past historical slave owners is now challenged to make a difference the country that once held us in bondage of slavery.

Scottish rulers of the past the dark rulers of the powers at the top now brought low in the chaos of our British parliament to know that we all huger for the food love and forgiveness irrespective to the colour of skin. The passports to freedom a package away from knowing that you are either British or remain to keep to your mother's background is an expensive price to pay to pay back to the movement for Black History and the Movement for Respiratory for justice to what has happed to our communise and social structures in the past breaking out from slavery mentality in our minds souls and spirts not just our hands and feet. Yes, we can do it we can fight on we can make a stand through the freedom of love peace and education our leaders standing for what is right and the juices of our social society irrespective of our backgrounds.

Our African background with the melody of the Caribean heart of love and freedom we are just understanding the Caribbean music to my ears to our social life. The African drums of music reminds me of not just of the kinship of rulers in dark places. I now appreciate the light of rulers shedding light not just my situation and circumstances from a historical factor breaking the chains of old traditional curses and practices instead of blessing others. We bless as God gives the blessings to whom he thinks without favourites only favour to all mankind. Does it not say God reigns on the Just and on the Unjust? I am sure I heard the preacher man say from the Holy Bible. I am proud to be black nothing wrong with black in the mysteries of his love of freedom his love for us. The Muslim book of instructions to life has been shared with heart of love from so many friends as we cross-culturally evanglised with respect to muslim beliefs with so much we ourselves have learned the value of good in a man or woman – the heart of love is to share. Thank you. – peace unto all men God bless you my friend. In simple humbleness we bless our friends with love so much good principles to learn from others.

We have faced up to our own weakness. To know that I must not give up the fight as Bob Marley has said to many right across the cultures of our global village. Respect yourself to try, respect yourself to succeed, respect yourself to love, make peace with love for fellow man to share a love and hope in a practical way to others. We must not give up our fight for freedom to a new dimension a new era of freedom – the road is ahead of us all

A cup of water, a smile, a meal, to someone shows you care to dying community children and adults. A better future for you with love and a better future for others with your tender heart of love. Not just in word but in deeds. Not just from pulpit preaching and teaching but understanding those that are different from what they believe. Understanding the heart, the mind and reaching out to others in the safe way. The human way, we have a heart of peaceful loving entering the spirits of society by our actions, not just in words. No more are we only govern by geographical rules but our prayers are lifted to the heavens celebration for total surrender the songs of praises over all our communities starting with Reading my home town.

A New Freedom

The freedom of voice in song, faith love and peace and helping others not only to faith but to rebuild a better community for ourselves. The momentous occasion of love and peace where we all hand in hand in our communities share love if not faith – we have a right to be different a right to choose the best path for lives. Forgetting the past slavery rulers of our towns with reminders of struggles of slavery years turning a town around to build love to all back grounds working together for a blessing.

Queen Victoria to a modern royal family, a modern society a modern political system, that embraces the needs of a changing Britain even after Brexit is long over – a mindset that challenges us all to be better and to defend our rights to a better life in our communities Black History Month (Are we in position to help ourselves more and UK....as we continue to make our stand as Black British citizens in modern Britain that is changing. More in Parliament is needed. We have a future…

Happy for Megan and her royal hubby, the baby will grow up and understand life as royal family member. Coming from a mixed race back ground understanding the black heritage and also the appreciating the freedom of the past now enjoying the life of king history with a future.

There is still honey in my night with moon lighting the shores of the Caribbean become the comfort listen to the seashores of love of comfort of my husband, our husbands your husbands our men. Our men need the love of a good woman more than ever before a man heartbreaks tender-hearted men with a bull head of exterior physics' knowing that the loss of a child a mother a wife a sister in the trails of destructions of the shores blowing winds of devastation and destruction.

The cry the voice of help is needed we can no longer look back to our history with regrets. We need to come together help our fellow communities as humans understanding with wisdom the cries of each community and social group with longing hearts to outreach to show cups of love to a dying and broken world …cups of Jesus in food drink clothing a smile money or friendship in a true and not in deception to be unravelled by deceit and corruption – a ideal world it will never be. I dare you to be the ideal person to help bring change to someone's life starting with yours and then others.

The miracles of sharing with others outreaching to those that are different with respect in a practical way goes a long way to any one in our community, the jobless the homeless the Humiliation of incest of a hurting daughter only to share the gospel of your truths in prison never to be free to hurt the tender-hearted of the daughter who once looked up to you for divine leadership. Don't allow your platform to be a step in the wrong direction. The turnaround is ready for us all to bring about a change to our own lives, and communities as we seek a better change a strong voice for the right and justice for our relationships and communities. Forgive, apologise, say sorry, embrace peace and love.

Letting go of the hand of bitterness and cruel pains injustice moving to a brighter future. Hold on to the hand of hope love and wisdom truth and justice for your life. The hour of freedom and happiness blessings and hope. The poisoned of hearts and minds to overspill into our communities needs to be healed from the deception of hatred and bitterness on the inside. The bridge to healing the social needs of our social hearts cry is to change. The outward looking eyes balanced with sense of expression to the inner heart of your heart. The dance of your heart back to happiness, cheer and the rhythm of the heartbeat of your inner laughter and smile to bring a smile to others to heal the pain of social injustice. Are we listening to our hearts of love

Prayer that Matters

A prayer for uncertain times based on the Second Sunday in Lent and St. Patrick's Day in United Kingdom,

'Do not be afraid, I am your shield; your reward shall be very great.' Genesis 15:1

'For he will hide me in his shelter in the day of trouble; he will conceal me under the cover of his tent; he will set me high on a rock.' Psalm 27:5

'Wait for the LORD, be strong, and let your heart take courage, wait for the Lord.' Psalm 27:14

'But our citizenship is in heaven, and it is from there that we are expecting a Saviour, the Lord Jesus Christ.' Philippians 3:20

'How often have I desired to gather your children together as a hen gathers her brood under her wings, and you were not willing.' Luke 13:34

New Rhythm

Push on forward as the rhythm of the African Drums play ISREAL OH LETS BE REAL with a singing heart full of melody of the one love tunes singing over Nigeria with Bob Marley's one love as I prepare for my own marriage from Basingstoke my king has come to capture my heart of love straight to Reading to brighten my path from day to day- oh how sweet it is to walk in this pilgrim way leaning on Gods arms of love – His ARC of love is real to me dancing the tunes of love from the Caribbean seas to the British waters as we both sail from London to St Lucia and St Vincent in the Arc of his love across the blue sun kissed seas making the sand beaches are beds to catch the sun. Who can fathom Gods love the sun God or the moon God or the God that made them all – our creator who knows us fearfully and wonderfully made – gifts and talents to share to the social society of our neighbours loving them as ourselves?

The breakthrough of the hand of Supreme God over all your matters will push you to the next level of your life …Putting on the whole Armour of God for he will stand for you in all your affairs that surround the inspirational relationships of God in the ARC of God's love – the shifting and the pruning to test the strength of your love– Justice and vengeance belongs to God alone, When others have wrong you, Arise and stand for your true potential to be the best you can ever be in your country.

New Hope of Joy

Forgiving the past never forgetting our history. A jump into the Light of the Future from the Darkness of Past of slavery now breaking free into a bright future for our Black communities working with others for a more positive future learning the lessons from the past. As we pass on the recipes of love to our next generation from Milton Keynes and open eyes of love for our future running through to London back over to Reading surely God is a God of love and not hate.

The British seas past filled with blood of the African and Caribbean slaves, now can we wash the guilt of bloodthirsty men of the past to rebuild a new community for our UK. A challenged and changed mentality to our country as the chains of the slavery mentality in both camps are broken – we are free ready to move on, move forward, aim high, push and pull our minds and gird ourselves with the truth knowing that God loves us all. Colour, Creed, Religion, Background, Political mindsets. We with God we are more than conquerors to break the chains that influence to harm others for the purpose of power only to bring destruction to a nation.

New Blessing

An arrangement has been made for a grand occasion, before arriving the UK. With my grandmother as they do in the days of historical blessings. Past present and future we meet again. Breaking the generation curses of old of the dark kingdoms of enquiry, we know that that God blessings on our lives marriages husbands and wives, we make no mistake of dark enquires of who to marry, where to live or where to work – what is on the cards nothing. We need not worry of the past of ancestry or our families, even if our wives or mothers was a witch or prostitute or a murder, the fact that God has placed you in such a family is for your blessing your benefit so be not afraid. On arrival to a cold UK with warm hearts to embrace and starting a new journey of family life – Gods Arc of Love on the sailing of the shores to a land in need of rebuilding. As we rebuild our land of past, we rebuild our land with the present and the future knowing that each generation is blessed with the mercies of love poured from the skies of the UK as the sun shines in the African and Caribbean lands.

We are a product of Gods vision and dreams. My dream has come true. I have done myself the favour of being obedient to God, honour your mother and father that the days may be long in the land that he has given you. God has given me the UK as my home. No matter how many times I go back to my ancestor home of Barbados in the Caribbean God goes before me and has blessed my life my family and the work of his hands of his beautiful island is blessed. Our islands are blessed as we travel from Africa to Caribbean to main land UK and Europe, no distance is too far to travel to see the making of a new dawn in our lives and families bringing hope to our generation and people As interesting as it sounds, historical evidence backgrounds and life in accordance to our black heritage, "Boris Johnson are you the slave master that once rule my father's family". As daring as this sounds it would be interesting to travel back in past times. Let's look to future knowing that we have far to go. The future is to face up to our visions together as we carry out our lives in a great county we now holding our country to the contrary of a knife edge of Brexit in Gods Arc of Love.

The 12th hour of our countries is this hour of need, may our reflections be with us all this Black History Month, we look at ourselves not our titles and names. With five golden rings to the call of the European Empire of the past, now the modern rulership of knowing that we have a great future ahead of us as people. We all belong to our God – God rules on the just and the unjust and loves us all.

Our history with a future – Black Lives Matters

We recognise the historical social issues of our great country. We move forward this October 2019, driving us to a greater and better future in our great UK Our Black population and issues can be resolved as we work together to bring out the best out of our Black Population making a mark in history to our future.

From Queen of Scots, to Prince of Wales, the Caribbean Queen Ship of our Island Barbados - sailing all over our Spanish, Dutch and French islands to the Old ship of Zion our Christian heritage - sailing across the Caribbean shores waving the banner of love and victory over our Islands as we celebrate the oneness of love regardless.

Our Countries, Black History has a future. Out of slavery, oppression and occultic black magic. The slavery to our white ancestors' rulership's. Breaking the chains off our minds, hearts, souls, families, finances, churches and counites we break every chain over our UK that will keep our Black Population in bondage to the past of slavery. Breaking the shame of knowing that it has happened is breaking the chains of our white minds. To face up to knowing that there is also freedom for you too. We both forgive and heal the pain of a great History no more in bondage but now in freedom. Yesterday has gone today we are in need.

The land is blessed our plantation land is blessed, no longer ruled by our former slave masters, the land of our forefathers the chains of the past has been broken, breaking every chain off the sea and land our great country and Islands are blessed, the old occultic practice of joining man and wife is broken – that old time religion no longer applies - no weapon formed Gods people shall surely prosper as we take the council from the Godly and not the Ungodly, that is only good enough for me, my Grandmother's generation, my mother's generation living the struggles of old breaking the mould for now my generation. Trick or Treat we treat others with love and respect. Bless the Lord all ye lands he psalms David has prayed to his God

"Many people worked here and many people died here," says Meno, the hotel's official nature guide and historian, who has taken us on a beguiling walk-through part of the 200-acre forest with frequent stops to savour the sights and sounds. Tasting the sweet, tangy, fleshy coating around a cocoa seed and inhaling an intense lemon balm smell from a crushed leaf opened a new array of natural notes are sensorial rhapsody.

The Islands treasure - St Lucia St Vincent and Barbados as one in no volcano disaster will separate the love of our islands and our people.

But it is the slave trade past, told with honesty, that arrests the soul.

"They would work all day, till they dropped and the ones that ran away would be captured and executed," adds Meno, a 54-year-old former local footballer, who has worked at

Anse Chastanet for almost 30 years. "They existed on a diet of bread fruit. They were allowed to worship once a week but some of them decided suicide was the best way out." A Castanet article I have read http://allaboutstlucia.com/history/ In March 1996, at a UWP convention, Compton lost the leadership, after 30 years, and was replaced as prime minister by Dr Vaughan Lewis. An early general election in May 1997 resulted in victory for the SLP, winning 16 of the 17 seats, with 61 per cent of the votes, and SLP leader Dr Kenny Anthony became prime minister. Lewis resigned as leader of the UWP, having lost his seat.

Our Islands that shines so bright with new hope for our future. Our dreams are now visions for others to see as we implement working together to bring the Light of Hope to a Great United Kingdom. Inspired truly to be the best lady I can ever be – Every woman every man can be the best they can be. A lesson learned over the years for our future. The Islands simply belong to God to take care of with his protective love over his people

Blessings and mercies from generation to generation on us all irrespective to our backgrounds – in the ARC of God's love in humbleness to a great God. Slavery is not doing what you should do, the freedom to choose to the right thing, and don't!

That is slavery modern day chains that hold you back the freedom to break though out of your hopeless to hope. A choice of freedom is to respect those in authority to bring freedom we found each other God brought us together and will lead us all through the success of past and present is simply a bright future in the Arc of God's Love – Inspirational Relationships

Celebrating successful women with likeminded women pushing through the storms of life. After the darkness of Covid comes the light of Hope and Success supporting international women
With Triamph
Svetlana Ratnikova
https://www.linkedin.com/in/svetlanaratnikova/members/

Sales, Marketing, Lead Generation and Networking. Skills and Strategies. Seminars.

Sisters Uncut was founded three and a half years ago in protest against Conservative austerity measures that have cut and <u>closed life-saving domestic violence support services</u> across the country (Bates, 2018). As domestic violence support workers and survivors, we've seen first-hand how this brutal removal of specialist support has left survivors trapped in danger. Since then, the situation has only got worse, and we have campaigned relentlessly to push the government to take state responsibility for keeping survivors safe. **Sisters Uncut (2018) 'Theresa May's bill is a distraction from the austerity cuts that have left support services crumbling and survivors in peril',** ***Guardian*****, 19 February**

Every Woman Every Man deserves to be loved

True Inspirations Heather Butcher

77

www.ingramcontent.com/pod-product-compliance
Lightning Source LLC
Chambersburg PA
CBHW051219250726
48655CB00006B/2500